Devil, You Can't Have My Family!

Devil, You Can't Have My Family!

by
Dwight Thompson

Harrison House
Tulsa, Oklahoma

Devil, You Can't Have My Family!
ISBN 0-89274-912-1
Copyright © 1993 Dwight Thompson Ministries
P.O. Box 1122
Downey, California 90240

Published by Harrison House, Inc.
P.O. Box 35035
Tulsa, Oklahoma 74153

Devil, You Can't Have My Family!

Contents

1   Get a Tough Holy Ghost Policy   11

2   Stand in the Gap   21

3   It's 10:00 — Do You Know Where Your Children Are?   35

4   Do You Want Your Kids To Be Just Like You?   47

5   Devil, You Can't Have My Children   61

6   Mama, Hold Onto God   67

7   Keep the Light On and the Table Ready   73

8   Train Your Children in the Way They Should Go   81

9   Choose To Influence Your Children for God   91

10   Now, Lead Them to the Lord   103

1
Get a Tough
Holy Ghost Policy

1
Get a Tough Holy Ghost Policy

You would be concerned if a man walked into your house and said, "I'm going to take your child from you." You would stand up and defend that child with your life. Isn't that right? Well, I want to encourage you right now to stand up and don't be passive about the spiritual well-being of your family. Forget that "whatever will be will be" idea. You believe for *your* salvation, don't you? When you get sick, you believe God for *your* healing, don't you? And if you're full of fear you know you can believe God to take that fear away from you and replace it with faith, can't you? I want you to do the same thing right now regarding your family. Your family is going to be saved.

Everyone reading this book has someone who needs God. Take your Bible right now, find Acts 16:31, and draw a circle around it.

And they said, Believe on the Lord Jesus Christ, and thou shalt be saved, and thy house.

That tells me that not only can I believe God for *my life* to be saved, but also I have a right to claim *my family*.

You say, "There is nothing I can do about my family; there is nothing I can do about my children." That's incorrect. There is something you can do about it because you are a child of God, and there are blessings pronounced upon a child of God. The child of God has rights. You have a biblical right to claim your children for God. The devil can't just come in and take your family any time that he wants to. You may think that he can; he may tell you that he can, but you have rights.

Now I want you to say out loud with force, with meaning, with fervor and with determination, *"Devil, get your hands off God's property. Devil, get your hands off my property. Get your hands off my children, my husband, my wife, my brother, my sister, my mother, my father and all my loved ones. I command it in Jesus' name."*

I'll never forget one night in Miami, Florida, a woman came up to me on the platform. She was a little, short, powerful-looking individual. You could tell she was a fireball. She said, "Hey, you; wait a minute!" I turned around just in time to see her say to a big man beside her, "Get on up here right now. I want him to meet you."

She walked up to me and said, "Glory to God, it works." Just like that. "Glory to God," she said, "it works. I heard you preach 'Devil, You Can't Have My Children,' and I decided to claim my husband and I wouldn't take no for an answer."

She asked me, "Do you see that man?" Now you couldn't miss anybody like him. He was about 6'3" and weighed at least 240 pounds. That man could bite the bumper off of a pickup. What I'm trying to tell you is that he was a rugged individual. But he was just standing there in a shy way while she told me what had happened.

She said, "I decided, 'God, either You're going to save him or I'm going to kill him.' He was the biggest bum that ever lived." She said that right in front of him. (If she thought I was going to side in with her calling him a bum, she was mistaken. You don't call anybody that looks like him a bum; you call him "Sir" or "Mister.") "I had thought about killing him. He beat me. He slapped me around."

He was a truck driver out on the road about ten days and then home about ten days. While he was home he drank, and everybody in the house had to leave. He was mean and obnoxious when he was drunk, she told me.

"I decided that instead of killing him, I was going to see him saved," she said. "So I got your tape on claiming your children. One night when he came in and was lying on that bed drunk, I started playing your tape. You said to call him into the kingdom; put faith into his heart in the name of the Lord. You said to speak Isaiah 54:13 over him.

> **And all your [spiritual] children shall be disciples — taught of the Lord [and obedient to His will]; and great shall be the peace and undisturbed composure of your children** (AMP).

"I said that about my husband. I didn't dare say anything to him while he was drunk, but when he was passed out — sometimes for two or three days — in spite of what I saw, I said, 'I don't care what it looks like, I will not lose my husband. Devil, he's not going to be lost, he's going to be born into the kingdom of God.'"

She said there were times he would be lying there in his own vomit, a mess. She would think *I'd like to kill him*, but she would say, "In the name of the Lord, husband, you are a disciple taught of the Lord, in obedience to the divine will of God and great shall be your peace and composure." She would talk right in his ear while he was asleep. When she'd get tired, she would turn on the tape recorder and I would preach for a while to him. She began to anoint his bed and his forehead.

One day when he came home — he had been getting meaner and meaner — she thought *Oh, here he comes again*, but suddenly the Spirit of the Lord came upon her and told her that something had happened, told her to begin to pray. He walked in with his sack full of booze, just like he did at the end of every ten-day trip, and he walked to the kitchen sink, never said a word, unscrewed the caps from all that whiskey and poured it down the sink. He ran over and picked up his little wife and said, "I've given my heart and my life to the Lord Jesus Christ. I've been saved."

"What happened?" she asked.

He said, "I was passed out." He had a job that kept him out for a long time with two or three days off between hauls. He would crawl up in the back of his truck and drink for those days. "I woke up looking for you. I heard your voice in my ear and you were saying things like, 'My husband shall be saved. He is a disciple taught of the Lord.' I kept hearing you talking so I got up, looked around, called your name and tried to find you; but I was a few hundred miles away from home and I couldn't find you. I went around the cab thinking *Where is my wife? I hear her praying.*"

That was deep in his spirit; it got into his spirit that he was a disciple taught of the Lord. That man fell down on his knees and gave his heart to God. God changed his life because one little wife made up her mind that her husband was going to be saved in the name of the Lord Jesus Christ and turned him over to God. Hallelujah!

She Loved Him Into the Kingdom

(The following story is about how one woman believed God to save her husband. If you are believing God to save your husband, do not allow yourself to be in the type of dangerous situations she did unless you're very sure the Holy Spirit is leading you to do so.)

I remember as a child, how my parents (my daddy was a Pentecostal pastor) in the middle of the night would take my brother and me over to the house of one of the ladies in the church, and my daddy would say we couldn't go in. "This is for adults; you're too young, so stay out here." When I became a teenager I found out what was going on: the man in that house used his wife as a punching bag. He was a drunken mean man, and she was a born-again Christian. She would come to church and sing in the choir. Sometimes she had to wear dark glasses because her husband had hit her in the face and blackened her eyes. He broke her nose twice. He took his frustrations out on her.

Still she praised and thanked God for her husband. She would say, "I just love my husband, John. I just love him, and God's going to save him."

Her parents told her, "Why don't you throw that bum out? He beats you. He's an adulterer and a bum." And he was. He was a certified bum. The guy was really something else. She had a legal claim to toss him out. She said, "I'm not going to do it. If God will save my husband because I love him and stick with him, then other people are going to believe that God can save their husbands. I'm going to love him into the kingdom of God." So she just kept loving him, for years she kept loving him, loving him, praying for him, claiming him, standing on the Word of God, claiming him, claiming him, claiming him for God!

One cold Wednesday night as she was preparing to go to prayer meeting, he was in a drunken stupor, playing with a revolver. He was cleaning his gun and loading it. He got mad at her because she was getting ready to go to prayer meeting. (He always got mad when she went to church.) As she was putting on her coat, she started for the door. He said, "Tonight I'm going to kill you."

She looked over at him and said, "I love you, John."

And he said, "I'm going to kill you tonight." She kept walking and singing. He said, "If you go any closer to the door, I'll shoot you." She reached out to touch the doorknob and he said, "If you touch that doorknob I'll blow your brains out."

She turned around and looked at him in a loving way and said, "John, I love you. John, if you pull that trigger, I'm going to go straight to heaven, but if you don't, I'm going to go to church." Isn't that wonderful? Isn't that something else? She went on to church! (But again, don't do something like this unless you're absolutely sure the Holy Spirit is leading you to do so.)

She hadn't been there long when someone came onto the platform and told my daddy there was an emergency at her house. The lady ran out with us and got in the car. Since I was a teenager now and had my driver's license, my daddy had me drive over to their place — the same place where I used to go but couldn't go in because it was for adults only.

We went inside. There was an emergency: her husband was on the linoleum floor in the kitchen crying out, "God, forgive me of all my sins. I'm an old mean sinner, and I want You to forgive me." This man had all his booze bottles with all the lids off turned upside down in the sink. When his wife walked in, he jumped up and hugged her, begged her forgiveness. After all those years of that woman standing up and saying, "I'm believing God to save my husband," that man gave his heart to the Lord Jesus Christ.

When he was asked what happened, he said, "If a woman could love me after all that has happened, I decided I would live for her God for the rest of my life." As far as I know, to this day, fifteen years later, he is filled with the Holy Spirit and going on with God. God will do the same for your husband.

We use a phrase now and then that we hear politicians use: *a get tough policy*. I'd like you to establish a get tough Holy Ghost policy in your life regarding the salvation of your loved ones. Quit taking those lies from the devil that he is going to kill them.

In the spirit, see them born again. Don't line up with what you see in the natural because that promotes fear. You cannot be in faith and fear at the same time; so in order to rebuke fear, you've got to stand in faith. Fear cancels faith, but faith cancels fear. If you line up with "Thus saith the Word of the Lord," in spite of what you see, in spite of every outward symptom, you will see them saved and not lost.

I don't see your family dying in their sins, but by faith I see them born into the kingdom of Almighty God. I see them saved in the name of the Lord Jesus Christ. I claim that they shall be saved. I see them as disciples taught of the Lord, in obedience to the divine will of God; great is their peace and their composure.

Fight in the Spirit for your families. Nehemiah gave words of encouragement and challenge:

> **Then as I looked over the situation, I called together the leaders and the people and said to them, "Don't be afraid! Remember the Lord who is great and glorious; fight for your friends, your families, and your homes!"**
> **Nehemiah 4:14 TLB**

2
Stand in the Gap

2
Stand in the Gap

The number one request in my office is this: "Pray for my lost loved ones." That is number one. Only a short time ago, a woman, at a rally in Phoenix, told me that she had just buried her son. She said, "Brother Thompson, I know where my son is tonight. My son is in hell. I know my son is in hell."

I'm going to expose Satan's plan right here. Have you ever wondered why Satan hates you? It's simple. He hates you because you are God's precious creation.

In the book of Genesis God said that the seed of the woman would bruise the head of the serpent. That seed, Jesus Christ, was born of a woman, and He mortally wounded the head of the serpent. That's the reason he hates the seed of the woman so much: that seed represented ultimate destruction of his entire kingdom. That's why he hates humanity.

Of course he cannot destroy God. He cannot destroy Jesus Christ, the Son of God. He cannot destroy you if you're born again, trusting in God and walking with God. So his next target, in my opinion, is the children — my children and your children.

I want to thank God both of my children are serving God. Both of them and their spouses are born-again people and are serving God. Still, Satan would like to steal and to destroy them; he would also like to destroy their children. He would like to destroy your children.

But I have some excellent and exciting news for you. While Satan's plan and Satan's goal is to destroy your family and to destroy your children and to do everything in his power to pull them down, God also has a plan. Hallelujah!

You need to realize that you do have something to say about it. Anybody who tells you that you can do nothing about your lost family has not spoken the Word of God. You are going to enter into a plan with God and fully expect that those who are lost are going to be found!

On December 7, 1970, I was standing in a room at the Owens Brumley Funeral Home in Fort Worth, Texas. Nobody was in that room but me and the remains of one I loved, my brother, Rex. He was my best friend. We were very close. December 5, at the age of twenty-nine years, he was involved in an automobile accident.Sunday morning, December 6, eleven hours, forty-five minutes later, in Tyler Memorial Hospital in Tyler, Texas, the doctor came from the room and said, "I'm sorry, he's gone." December 8, we had his funeral.

But on December 7, I was standing in Owens and Brumley Funeral Home. I walked over and closed the door. I wanted to be alone with my thoughts. As I sat in a chair beside the remains of my brother, my mind went back to when Zonelle and I were first dating. I had rebelled against God. I was far from God. I was breaking the hearts of my parents. I loved them deeply, but I wanted to live my life and I wanted to do it my way.

All of these years, as far as I know, my brother, for the most part, had led a good life. If there was ever one calling he had, it was the call of intercession. I sat in that room and thought about how God used my brother to snatch me from hell.

My brother told me these details long after the events I'm going to share with you had taken place. "Dwight, one night the Lord awoke me and suddenly I saw you dying in a car wreck. From that car wreck you were going into hell, and I literally saw the flames of hell. Immediately the Lord spoke to me and said, 'If you don't stand in the gap for Dwight, he's going to hell.'" That was an act of mercy for God to tell my brother that, because God works through His people.

"Dwight," he said, "I saw you in hell. Immediately I woke up and the sweat was pouring off my face. It was about 3:30 in the morning; I raced into your room and you were not there. I fell down next to your bed and asked God, 'Does this mean that my brother is already in hell?' God said, 'No, he's out and he's away from Me right now; but if you will hold on to Me on his behalf and stand in the gap I will save him.'" That's what Rex told me later.

My brother entered into a covenant with God. He said, "I will hold onto God until Dwight is saved. I will pray until he gives his heart to God. He will not rest." He told me, "I made up my mind, 'Dwight, you're not going to rest. The Holy Spirit conviction is on your trail. You're not going to enjoy being in this house, because I'm going to pray you into the kingdom.'"

My brother was a weight lifter and he had won several trophies in his class for weight lifting. He could do anything he wanted to. I didn't dare test it too much unless I had a 2 x 4 or a crowbar. And I think he could have bent the crowbar in two. I'm glad I never found out.

I will always remember that first night my brother prayed. I came in at about 4:00 a.m. There was nothing but one wall and a squeaky door between our two rooms. That night when he prayed, he was unusually loud.

My brother had massive hands. When he would get anointed, he seemed to enjoy taking those hands that looked like hams and banging on something. Call it emotion or whatever you want to, but his prayers got answered. I can still see him in church praying. He had a low baritone voice that could get louder than mine. (And I'm pretty loud as you know if you've heard me preach.) When he would pray at my dad's church sometimes, he would bring his hand up and bang it down on the altar. Heads would bob up and down on that altar.

Rex would wait until he heard the door squeak as I came in. I would be tired and lie down. He would give me just enough time to get comfortable and he would start praying. That boy would pray, most of the time, for two to three hours. Since I didn't get in until three o'clock in the morning, we didn't get much sleep.

He would always start praying using a vocabulary second only to Webster. (He was the second highest in his graduating class in one of the largest universities in Fort Worth, Texas.) He could use so many words that I didn't even know what he was talking about. Then, when he clicked in with the Holy Ghost, his praying took on a spiritual brute force. He would pray and beat the wall or hit the door...while I was trying to sleep! I covered my head with pillows and that didn't help. Every picture in the house would be crooked in the morning. This went on for one, two, three, four nights.

What I didn't know then was that he had made up his mind he was going to log each day and the number of hours he prayed for however many days it took. He was a guy who liked to keep records. He had been that way all his life.

You have to make an unqualified commitment to God that you are going to love your family into the kingdom of God and hold on to the horns of the altar in intercession, standing in the gap for them. (Ezek. 22:30.) Usually one person in the family will be saved, then they will stand in the gap of the hedge for the others. A gap-stander will make up the hedge.

God setteth the solitary [one person] **in families: he bringeth out those which are bound with chains** (Ps. 68:6) and He leads them out through prayer. Pray the Word. Speak the Word. Noah prepared the ark for the salvation of his "whole house."

What does that mean, "standing in the gap"? That's what Abraham did for Sodom. (See Gen. 18.) Abraham asked the Lord if He would spare Sodom if He could find fifty righteous men there. God agreed. There weren't fifty righteous there. Abraham asked for forty...finally down to ten. But there were not ten righteous men in Sodom. God remembered Abraham, though, and spared Lot. God sent angels in and they took Lot by the hand and jerked him out of that place and the same day fire and brimstone fell upon that city. (Gen. 19:16-23.)

Even on the very day fire and brimstone comes on this world, I believe God will pull your loved ones to safety. The devil has lied to you and shown you your family dying in their sins. I don't see them dying in their sins. I see them coming to God.

For ninety days Rex Thompson prayed for his brother, Dwight Thompson. I got so mad at that boy that there were times I threatened to go in his room and take him on. (I said I got mad but I was not insane. It just wasn't a good idea.) He'd go in his room and pray through that squeaking door. That got so old. Can you imagine coming in at nearly daylight — the only chance you're going to get to sleep is a few hours — and your brother starts praying for you? In his baritone voice he would pray loud and long, beating on the wall until the windows shook. I was going bananas in my room.

He was praying and praying and I was trying to sleep. It was hard to do. I told my mother some mornings, "We've all had pretty good peace in this house. But if you don't tell Rex to quit that praying and quit bugging me at night I'm going to go in there and punch him out."

I can still hear my mother saying, "Dwight, we taught you not to fight. Don't you talk that way about your brother. He loves you." Under her breath all the time she was one of the conspirators saying, "Go Rex, go, go."

During this time, I was driving back and forth to Dallas courting Zonelle. I wasn't getting much rest. I worked all day and then drove to Dallas every night to see Zonelle. On the way home one night, while driving on the Dallas-Fort Worth Turnpike, I fell asleep at the wheel. My car ran into the back of a large truck. The roof of the car was sheared completely off; the steering wheel was cut in half; all the glass was shattered out of the windows; the rear view mirror cut my forehead. The car swerved, and the miracle was I should have been thrown against the driver's side, but instead I landed on the floor of the passenger's side. A narcotic agent was driving in a car right behind mine. He witnessed the terrible accident and ran to my car to help. As he leaned into the car, he was amazed to find me fully conscious. "Son," he said, "you're supposed to be dead." Everyone there insisted I go to the hospital, but I was released when all they found was a small gash on my forehead and a few cuts on my hand. No doubt the devil was definitely trying to kill me to stop the future ministry I was called to, but in the spirit world warfare was taking place for my soul because, in my home, my brother was praying.

While I was sitting there in that funeral home looking at my precious brother's remains, all this was going over in my mind. That boy prayed ninety days and nights. He held on to God for me. He stood in the gap. I was on the road to hell but my little brother stood in the gap for his brother. He prayed and prayed. Some nights I'd be in there and I'd say, "God, he's driving me crazy."

Every morning when I'd get to the table, if I showed up for breakfast — he would have been praying all night and would have kept me up all night — he would come in there and bang my shoulder and say, "How are you doing, Dwighty?"

I'd say, "Fine." He just kept praying and praying.

I finally told my dad, "Dad, I've got rights in this house. I am afforded rights of peace. You make Rex shut up and quit all that praying."

He said, "Son, if the Lord has led your brother to pray, you never want to interrupt God." My daddy was in on it, too. The whole bunch was in on it! That kid prayed and prayed.

When You Stand in the Gap, Something Is Going To Happen

My brother had prayed for me for ninety days. On the ninetieth day, he opened the door and started praying. He'd start low with that beautiful baritone voice. Then he moved off into this other thing. I didn't mind the intellectual praying. But when he got off into the Spirit, praying in this heavenly language, and beating on the wall, that was too much.

He told me at times he literally wrestled demons and devils. It sure sounded like it to me because it sounded like bodies slamming against the wall. He nearly broke the hinges off the door. I really believe he was fighting demons off my soul. Thank God for my little brother. He prayed and prayed.

That ninetieth day he started praying and beating on the wall, and all of a sudden he just quit. That made me raise up in bed and think, "What's happened? After all these nights am I really going to get a night's rest?"

Then I heard him sobbing heavily. He was carrying many hours in college. He was having to cram and work;

and then when I came in he was having to start his praying. Then he'd have to go to school all day. Among all of it, he carried me. He carried my soul. He refused to let Satan have my soul.

That night he cried and this is what he said (I heard him say these words), "Oh, God, I told You I will not stop praying until You save Dwight, but I really am tired. I do need a little encouragement. Would You save him kind of in a hurry? But I will pray until he is saved if it takes me the rest of my life."

That night I learned how prayer worked. Something came over me so strong that I cannot explain it to you. All I remember is I felt conviction in my soul. I was at the end of my road. Suddenly my sins were crying out against me and I cried out, "Oh, God, I need You."

I began to cry out, lying on that bed, fully clothed. I hadn't even gotten ready for bed. That night I cried out, "God, forgive me." That night every light in the house went on. My mom and dad came roaring in there and my brother came in there. I was crying out to God like a house on fire.

And my little brother came in. He was 45" in the chest and he had a 29" waist; his forearm measured 19". He could military press over 360 pounds (that's standing up and snapping it over your head like it was a match stick.) He came in there and I was praying out to God. The lights were on. It was daylight. My brother put his arms around me and squeezing me said, "That's it, Dwighty, tell it to God."

He got me up out of bed. I was on my feet. I was standing up and he was standing behind me. I cried out, "Oh, God, save me." When I said that, he squeezed me — cut off my wind and made me feel like every rib was breaking. I thought, *He prayed me into the kingdom and to make sure I don't backslide, he is going to kill me so I go straight to heaven.* He loved me so much and I'm sure glad. He had his arms around me and he picked me up off the floor like I was a doll, and shouted and danced. He said, "Praise Him, Dwighty, praise Him."

I finally said, "Daddy, tell him to turn me loose. He's going to break my ribs." We were all praising the Lord together. God heard and answered my brother's prayer. My brother made a commitment to God and he would not let my soul go to hell. He stood in the gap for his brother for ninety days. That's why I'm preaching the Gospel now: I had a praying brother who held onto God on my behalf.

I stand in the gap with you, for your sons and daughters, in Jesus' name.

Remember what Job 22:22-30 says as you pray for others:

Verse 22

Receive, I pray thee, the law from his [God's] **mouth, and lay up his words in thine heart.** [Receive God's Word — lay it up in your heart.]

Verses 23,24

If thou return to the *Almighty* [El Shaddai — the God Who is more than enough], **thou shalt be built up, thou shalt put away iniquity far from thy tabernacles.**

The following is the result if you come to the Lord; you receive His Word; you put away sin far from your life.

Then shalt thou lay up gold as dust, and the gold of Ophir as the stones of the brooks.

God says if you put iniquity away from you, you will begin to prosper in all areas of your life.

Verses 25-27

Yea, the Almighty [El Shaddai] **shall be thy defence** ["defence" here has to do with gold in the Hebrew] **and thou shalt have plenty of silver.**

For then shalt thou have thy delight in the Almighty, [El Shaddai] and shalt lift up thy face unto God.

Thou shalt make thy prayer unto him, and he shall hear thee, and thou shalt pay thy vows.

If you lift up your face to the God Who says, "I'm more than enough," you're going to pay your vows — no matter what you've committed to God — you're going to do it.

Verse 28

Thou shalt also *decree* a thing, and it shall be established unto thee: and the light shall shine upon thy ways.

Decree here means "snatch."[1] You shall snatch a thing and it shall be established unto *you*.

Verse 29

When men are cast down, then thou shalt *say*, There is lifting up; and he shall save the humble person.

People will tell you they have everything materially, but they are not happy. They are cast down. You shall say there is hope for you, a lifting up.

Verse 30

He shall deliver the island of the innocent: and it is delivered by the pureness of thine hands.

AMP

He will even deliver the one [for whom you intercede] who is not innocent; yes, he will be delivered through the cleanness of your hands.

---

[1] James Strong, *The Exhaustive Concordance of the Bible* (Nashville: Abingdon, 1890), "Hebrew and Chaldee Dictionary," #1504.

What makes your hands clean? What makes you a righteous man? Jesus **is made unto us...righteousness...** (1 Cor. 1:30). When we put iniquity away from our tabernacle, repent of our sins and say, "I am the righteousness of God in Christ Jesus," then we can come before the Father and claim our unsaved loved ones. God says, "Because of the pureness of your hands I will deliver that island of people that belong to you." We can snatch our loved ones out of the devil's hands and win them into the kingdom of heaven.

> **And that they may come to their senses [and] escape out of the snare of the devil, having been held captive by him, [henceforth] to do His [God's] will.**
>
> **2 Timothy 2:26** AMP

> **...The harvest is indeed plentiful, but the laborers are few. So [I] pray the Lord of the harvest to force out and thrust laborers into His harvest** [and bring them across _____'s path].
>
> **Matthew 9:37,38** AMP

3
It's 10:00 —
Do You Know
Where Your Children Are?

3
It's 10:00 —
Do You Know
Where Your Children Are?

"I lived in a house all my life but never a home," a woman once said. "Tell the mothers of America to build a home where God lives supreme."

I heard a story that Daniel Webster, at the funeral of George Washington said, "If factories and fields are demolished, future generations will replenish them. If young capitol buildings are burned to the ground, at another time we can build them up. But who can restore the fabric of demolished homes?"

It seems like every time I turn around I see a young person who comes up to me and says, "I can't cope with life anymore. Can you help me?"

The other night when I sat at the table with my family, maybe that was on my mind; maybe it was just one of those times; maybe it was that I needed to be reassured as a father, and I'm honest with you, maybe I wanted my children to say to me, "Dad, you've been a good dad." Maybe that's what I wanted. I looked at my son and my daughter and asked them some questions, because I wasn't in any mood to take a chance.

We raised our children in church. We started the ministry when my daughter was two weeks old. We set them in the car and drove from revival to revival. They were raised in bassinets in the back seats of cars, cheap motel rooms, Sunday school rooms in some churches and any place people would put us. That's how they grew up.

Could it be that I have been so busy in the ministry, that I've not been a good parent, that I've forgotten my children? What good would it be to me if I preached and Los Angeles came to God and I lost my son? Or I lost my daughter? All I could think about was that my boy was getting ready to go back to college from spring break. I wanted him to tell me if there was anything that we needed to talk about. Was there any problem? Was he hurting? Was there something on the inside; was he facing a battle? Had I presented myself to him as a man on a platform who preaches to people or am I the same man in private that I am in public? Do you understand? I wanted to know where my kids were.

The world is a pressure cooker. The pressures of conformity are overwhelming. Many kids today cannot find the answers they need and the help they need in the home, because homes today have changed drastically. There has never been an institution under attack by a cynical satanic society like the home is now. Please never forget that God had a home even before He had a Church. God considers the home very important.

When I think of home I think of Mother and I think of Dad and I think of a simple house and a lot of love. I think of the family table without the television set on. In the first place we didn't have a television for most of our lives, and in the second place, my mother wouldn't let us watch it at the table during meals. Mother required us to talk.

What do you say for one hour to somebody you've lived with all your life?

We just looked at each other and watched each other grow...and we talked. She wanted us to talk, to have a good time at the table. If we didn't, she'd take us aside into another room, correct us, send us back to the table saying, "Now, go in there and have a good time." That's the way it worked. That's the way we grew up. Today every time I go back to the simple, little frame house that I was raised in, all the memories are good because I know they loved me there.

In today's society everybody is uptight. The parents are concerned because the economy has gone crazy. It seems as though most people have to hold down two jobs in order to pay the bills. The unfortunate thing about that is it leaves the children alone to figure out life for themselves. It seems like the dad works the day shift, the mom works the night shift and the kids have to learn to shift for themselves. The television has become the baby sitter. As a result, the children figure out for themselves what they can do with a lot of time on their hands. One psychologist said it is that time that often leads them to experiment with drugs, sexual experiences or alcohol.

One kid told me, "Life is simply a bummer. I don't know who I am, what I am doing on this planet or where I am going."

Parents, I want you to know where the kids are coming from. Kids today are not totally to blame. I'm not much in favor of getting up and yelling at kids and saying, "It's your fault you've turned out like you have." That's not the case. Kids today are hurting. They don't know where to turn. They don't even know to whom they can turn. The kids are searching, and they hurt deeply inside. They want to know someone loves and cares for them.

We live right now in a society that thinks it's very cool for our kids to get involved in drugs and alcohol. They're turning to drugs today because, as one kid said, "This is the only way I can get out of my trouble, escape the inner pain." In one high school alone it was estimated that over thirty-three percent of those high school students were experimenting with drugs.

The Decade of Rebellion

I feel that the decade of the sixties has already proven to be the most detrimental decade in modern history. The sixties introduced the Beatles' music to America. I have a right to my opinion and you have a right to yours. But since this is my book, I'll give you my opinion.

Stop and look closely at what took place in the sixties when these very talented English young men came to America. There is no question of their talent, their great musical ability. They certainly exceeded the field for many years. But the problem was the lyrics of many of the songs that the Beatles and other acid rock groups began to introduce were blasphemous and filthy.

The youth began to dance to the downbeat of satanic music. They began to sing the lyrics of satanic songs: songs that depicted Christ as anything but the holy Son of God, songs that incorporated four-letter words in the musical lyrics. They used lyrics that blasphemed and mocked God.

At the same time the youth began to listen to that music, they began to experiment with drugs. The acid rock music and the drugs went together. I have actual film and slides of acid rock festivals across America. I have documentation from young people stating it was as easy to secure drugs at a rock festival as it was to buy aspirin in a drug store. Young people, a quarter of a million strong, would go to places like the Macon Rock Festival and many of them then would become involved in illicit drugs and immoral activities.

Young people, read this very closely. I'm not preaching down to you; I'm trying to alert you and to point out to you very specific dangers that are involved in turning away from God and rebelling against God. Everything that glitters is not gold. Satan always has a way of wrapping his materials and his devices in the most attractive and alluring packages. The most deadly poisons are often very sweet to the taste, but extremely lethal.

When my son was about two, I thought it was so cute when he would get up and start doing "The Twist" to the acid rock music that was playing. What I didn't know, but I did find out, was that satanic lyrics were packaged in the high shrilled music of acid rock. The music was very attractive, and it could become a habit that was difficult to break. The young people began to sing songs that were damaging not only to their minds, but to their bodies and to their spirits. As a result, almost an entire generation of young people were involved extensively in drugs, sang and danced to the downbeat of acid rock music with dirty, filthy, blasphemous lyrics and rebelled against authority. Lawlessness began to abound.

We saw in that decade the home begin to fragment: the divorce rate climbed and the number of single parents grew to almost epidemic proportions. In that same time, prayer was banned in the public schools. I point that out for a very specific purpose. When you quit praying things begin to happen. Whether the whole country was praying in school or not is really immaterial. It was symbolic of one thing: our youth were troubled. The biggest foot the devil had ever gotten inside the door to destroy our young people was successful in the years of 1960 to 1970: the Vietnam War broke out. Our kids were taught to tear up their draft cards. Riots took place at Kent State. We saw campus rebellion throughout the world.

They've Done It All

The lifestyle today that Hollywood paints for our children is one that is totally despicable according to the Scriptures. It used to be that if a girl was not a "virgin" it was something that she tried to hide, something she was ashamed of. But in today's free society, as a result of the sixties, young people have been taught through television and through movies that there is a new lifestyle and a new morality.

In a news magazine article I read not long ago, I read things that did more than trouble me, they made me break down and cry. This is old hat to all of us; we're so used to hearing it, we almost have a hard time letting our feelings get involved; but we should reach deep within the pit of our stomach, and digest it with emotion.

The magazine's reporters secretly interviewed boys and girls in a high school and a junior high school. They discovered that young people are taught today, in one fashion or another, that it's the "in thing to do" to be involved in premarital sexual activity. At the senior high school, some of the reporters found seven out of ten of the young ladies interviewed admitted to having premarital sex.

Then the ones who were virgins did not want them to know it. One girl after another said, "The reason I don't want anybody in this school to know that I'm not having sex with somebody is because they'll make fun of me. They laugh and ridicule and act like there's something wrong with you."

Again I realize that this is just the way it is today. "Everybody is doing it" is the old cliche we used to use years ago. But the devil has succeeded in destroying the morals not only of many of our youth, but even of the standards of something called "decency" that we used to be taught in the home.

Psychologists and psychiatrists have interviewed girls at age thirteen who boast of having sex with as many as five or six boys in one evening. An eleven-year-old girl talked about having sex when she was ten because of the peer pressure that was put on her.

Young people today don't think anything about it and it's no wonder. It's become a lifestyle. It isn't an experience that someone happens to have in the back seat of an automobile. It is something that most parents are aware of. One psychologist said the attitude now of the average parent is, "If that's the way it is, I just don't want my kid to embarrass me." The mother gives her daughter the prescription for birth control pills that she takes.

When the psychiatrists started interviewing the young people who were involved in drugs and alcoholism, which was over thirty-six percent of the student body in one high school alone, these young people began to talk of their sexual frustrations. They began to say, "We've already done it all, had it all. We've had the drugs, the booze, the sex. There's nothing else to experiment with." So what do they do? They get more heavily involved in drugs and alcoholism. They keep seeking but never finding. They keep experimenting. They've got to have different kinds of sexual activities, all types of kinky sex, weird, stupid, immoral, animalistic types of sex.

They've done it all. The kids at thirteen know more about the facts of life than most parents do at forty, because they've been educated by a society that has a rule that says no holds are barred. What is the outcome? They're now frustrated. They've done it all. They've got to have a higher kick.

They start dropping acid, LSD, smoking pot or taking other drugs. Acid is a great mind-expanding drug. They are supposed to be able to think with greater depths because their mind expands. Then they hallucinate. They begin to see rainbows and iridescent colors. These drugs will make them think with greater depth and degree than ever before. But, soon they have awful flashbacks. I've seen young people who have flashbacks and they start gnawing at their tongue. Or they start screaming out demonic sounds. Or they think they're common mongrel dogs; they run around on all fours. One girl, Linda, gave her testimony in a meeting we had. She thought that people were after her. She took a .22 revolver and put it to her temple because she thought that was the only way to get out of the torment. She pulled the trigger, but miraculously it was a faulty .22. After a several-hour operation, she lived, even though the bullet had penetrated the skull.

Linda said, "As I got involved in the hallucinating drugs, pretty soon instead of seeing the bright lights and beautiful colors I began to see monsters. I could see monsters crawling in my mind. I had flashbacks. Instead of having great memories of the first excitement and thrill of this high like I'd never had before, I saw grotesque monsters coming at me and pulling at me until I couldn't stand it anymore."

That's the same drug that caused Art Linkletter's daughter to jump out of an eighth-floor penthouse window, because she couldn't deal with the awful flashbacks.

Young people hear about the joy and excitement of a mind-expanding drug but they aren't told about the flashbacks that go with it. Pretty soon they start taking uppers and downers; and then they start snorting cocaine; but cocaine being a rich man's drug, they can't afford it for very long, so they go on up to heroine and start shooting it.

But it leaves a long trail of debris...of human garbage...wasted lives. Young people at sixteen, seventeen and eighteen have done it all, and they have nothing else to offer anybody. They say, "If this is what life is all about I don't want it." They become broken and emaciated and tortured.

When they go home and their parents learn about these activities, new problems develop. Pressures become greater in the home. Soon the parents are telling them, "Just stay out of trouble. Stay out of my hair. Leave me alone."

I'm not trying to blame the parents and I'm not trying to blame the child; I'm telling you that there is a very dangerous, lethal, sinister, satanic spirit that has been unleashed upon our society.

The thief comes only in order that he may steal and may kill and may destroy. I came that they may have and enjoy life, and have it in abundance — to the full, till it overflows.

John 10:10 AMP

We all know what is happening and it's all old hat, and nothing is new that I'm writing about — except when it happens to you.

Do you know where your children are? Do you know where they are in their mind, in their spirit, where they are literally, right now?

Let's don't take any chances with our kids. Let's know where our kids are. Don't wait until they get in trouble to pour out that affection and love on them; let's have a little preventive maintenance working all the time. Let's not take any chances right now.

Even if you can say, "Thank God, all my kids are saved," don't take that for granted. Stay brushed up on telling your children, "Hey, we're going to make it. Do you need anything? Is everything all right?"

Kids, go to your parents and say, "I want you to know that I love you."

4
Do You Want Your Kids
To Be Just Like You?

4

Do You Want Your Kids To Be Just Like You?

The kid starts out saying, "I want to be just like my dad." An anti-cigarette smoking commercial has come out showing a man walking along the road with a little boy right beside him. Then the man kicks a rock, and the little boy kicks the rock too. The man puts his arms behind him and walks, and the little boy puts his arms behind him and walks. The man sits down beside a tree and the boy sits beside him. He wants to be just like dad. Then it shows dad reach down and open a pack of cigarettes and put one in his mouth and smoke it. The pack of cigarettes is lying there. The little boy picks up a cigarette and puts it in his mouth. "Dad, do you want your son to be just like you?"

Do I want my son to be just like me? For years, the only place kids knew they could go to get help was home, but they can't seem to go there quite as much anymore because everybody is so busy. Many are home alone.

If there were ever one thing that caused me concern, it would be that the day would come when I would have to look in the face of my children and say, "I've failed you. I haven't loved you." At times it's made me get up in the middle of the night. Have I become too busy, am I too involved trying to reach people for God that I haven't been a good father in my home?

There is a force that is trying to get all of our priorities messed up: the home, the parents, the kids. But you and I are going to have to come to grips with this now. Our kids are doomed unless somebody in the home stands up for God. A dad can't say to the kid, "Son, don't smoke that marijuana," while he's sitting there sipping his can of beer or drinking his five-dollar bottle of scotch.

One boy told me, "I'm getting sick and tired of feeling the fist of my father in my face slugging me for smoking marijuana but we put him to bed totally drunk about three times a week." Kids are not going to stand for the hypocrisy anymore. They're not going to stand for the phonies anymore.

It's no wonder the kids today go and find drugs and alcohol, because they feel the pressure of a society that's gone absolutely mad. They don't understand what's happening.

One girl said to me, "I've lived my whole life in my home and my dad told me to do this and do that and my mother said, do this and do that. They said 'Do as I say, not as I do.' They spanked me until my legs were red and then they would put me on the Sunday school bus. They made me go to church, but they would stay home and drink beer and watch television. The next Sunday I would cry because I wanted them to go with me, but they would spank me and put me back on the church bus. I went more than once to my parents and asked them to lead me to God and tell me how to pray, but they said it was the church's responsibility."

I can take you to that girl today. For seventeen years her parents spanked her and made her go to church, but they never took her. Unless something has changed in the last year, that girl, at the age of thirty-three is walking the streets of New Orleans as a prostitute.

Parents, it's not enough for you to turn to your pastor and say that it's the pastor's job to lead your kid to God. It isn't enough to put clothes on their back, to put food in their stomach, and buy them a new sports car and send them to the finest colleges. There is a sinister force that is battling for the lives and minds and consciences and hearts and souls of our children. It's going to take more than putting them on a Sunday school bus. Thank God for the ones who have been saved because they were put on a Sunday school bus. I want you to know it is not enough, though. The devil is trying to kill them and to destroy them.

It's time that we parents rededicate our lives to a lifetime proposition of not *telling* our child what to do but to *being an example* to that child because our life speaks louder than our words.

I was raised with a young boy and his two brothers. We grew up in the same church. These three boys were raised in a home that was full of hard discipline. If they didn't go to church, it wasn't unusual for their dad to hit them in the face and beat them up. These boys were brought to church and often literally slammed on the front seat as their dad would sit there threatening them within an inch of their life if they didn't listen to the preacher. But the minute they got home the dad was anything but a godly father. As a result all three of those boys — if I've heard it once I've heard it probably a hundred times — said, "I can't wait until I become a man so I can whip my father for the way he has treated us."

Bridge the Gap

It isn't enough for us to tell our kids something we think they ought to do. The generation gap is caused because when the problems set in, we can't seem to sit down and talk. We can't seem to find a mutual ground. A communication gap develops.

I found out one thing that bridges that communication gap, that generation gap...and that's called l-o-v-e! When love rules that home you can sit down, one with another.

Dad, you don't have to understand that kid. You don't have to understand him or the way he is living. You don't have to understand the way he thinks. But there is one thing that child will understand and it's love. Kids understand love.

There has been more than one time that I've had to go to my children, sit down, look at them and with tears in my eyes I've had to tell them, "I've been wrong. I'm out of line. You were not wrong, but I was wrong. I want you to forgive me, and let's pray for me that God will help me."

You ask, "Dwight, you mean to tell me you did that? You made a statement like that?"

Yes, more than once I've had to do that. I've had to tell my children, "I'm kind of uptight and I shouldn't have yelled at you, and I want you to forgive me." I've never yet had my children fail to accept that. Instead, they put their arms around me and we all have a good cry together. The communication stays open.

I had a parent walk up to me and say, "Here's my kid. She's fifteen years old and pregnant. I'm embarrassed. What am I going to do?"

Yet, I know a true story of a mother in a distant town in Texas who wouldn't bring her daughter to church. She taught her daughter how to hold a cocktail glass, how to dress in a seductive manner, how to make the cutest little enticing statements; but she didn't teach that child how to live for God. When the girl got in trouble, the first thing the mother did was to come and blame the preacher. "It's your fault," she said. "Why didn't you tell my daughter?"

You cannot lay the responsibility of your child at the door of the church. You've got to be the spiritual priest of your home.

"Honey, I'm Proud of You"

There is a woman whom all of us know. She told me I could share her story. As a young child this girl was dedicated to Christ. Although her father, a preacher, loved her, she broke his heart. She grew up living a life of rebellion. When she went to college, she made a mistake that resulted in her being turned out of school. She felt she had embarrassed her parents and couldn't go home, but she called them.

She talked to her daddy. "Daddy, I've been thrown out of college; I've brought shame to your name and I've grieved you. I want you to forgive me. I want to know if it's all right if I come home."

Her daddy said, "Better than that, I'm going to come straight to you." That daddy got in his car and drove from Georgia to Springfield, Missouri. He walked in, put his arms around his daughter, took her back home and they knelt together and prayed.

This girl said, "I realized I had made a mistake; I had gotten out of line and done things I was ashamed of. My daddy said, 'Honey, it's forgiven. It's under the blood. You don't have to worry about it anymore. I'm not holding it against you.'"

Her dad was a high official in their denomination. The next week he was going to preach at a youth meeting and he asked her to go with him. She didn't know why he would want her to go, but she consented. All during the drive her dad would say, "I love you, darling; you look so beautiful and I'm so proud of you." The girl wondered why in the world he would be proud of her after what she'd done.

When they got to the meeting she didn't want to go in because everybody knew she had been kicked out of college. She wondered what everybody thought. Her dad asked her to come in, so she went in and sat on the back row.

He got up and opened his Bible. "Before I preach today," he said, "I want someone whom I love very much and of whom I am very proud to stand up." She knew he was talking about her so she stood up there at the back row. "This is my daughter. Look how beautiful she is. I want you to know I'm so proud of her; I want everybody to look at her." The whole crowd turned around, and her dad was beaming with joy.

The whole crowd knew she had been thrown out of college. But this dad did not reject her.

That girl has grown into a wonderful, godly woman, and her name is Jan Crouch. She said to me, "Dwight, I know I would be in hell now; I would not be doing what I'm doing if my father and mother had not forgiven me. They not only forgave me, but they forgot it. And from that time until the day my daddy passed away, he never one time brought up what I had done. He just loved me. He picked me up when I was in the pit. He said, 'Baby, you're always going to be my baby, and I'm always going to love you.'"

There is one thing you've got to do, Dad and Mom: you've got to forgive your kids for making mistakes. I don't care how many mistakes they've made. I don't care how they've embarrassed you, how many wrong things they've done, how much reproach they've brought to your name; the only friend they've got in the world is you.

That guilt feeling has got to be taken away. You've got to look at them and tell them that they're going to make it. Tell them, "Sure you made a mistake but we've all made them. Now get on your feet; we're going to go on with God. Keep getting up and you're going to make it." Keep telling them they're going to make it.

Young person reading this book, I love you. I don't care how many mistakes you've made. I don't care how deep in sin you are, and I don't care what you've done. I want you to know that Jesus Christ loves you. I love you. I don't condemn you. You're going to make it.

Let's Start Over From Here

You say, "Dwight, I've made too many mistakes as a parent. I wish I could turn back the clock. I wish I could live my life over in raising my children." Don't be so hard on yourself. We've all made mistakes; we've all done things we're ashamed of. See, parents suffer from guilt too, not just kids.

I know you, Dad, you look at your children, now grown. There's not a lot of communication anymore. Maybe your kids are already high school students. You look back at the days when they were born and you played ball with them in the yard. You took them to the circus or the zoo. You did good things with them, but through the years it all changed. The joy is gone. Now you look back and say, "I can't go back. Dwight, you say I ought to forgive my kid, but my kid's got to forgive me."

Kids are pretty forgiving, Dad. This may go against your pride but if you want out of that guilt trip you're on, you're going to have to be willing to look at your children and say, "I'm sorry. I've been out of line. I'm wrong."

I found out that young people know a lot about real love. They know a lot about forgiveness. They're waiting right now for their dad to put his arm around them and have that dad say, "I'm sorry that I have lived the way I've lived."

To the young person reading this book, I want you to know that it also is your responsibility to go to your parent and say, "I forgive you and I want you to forgive me."

When those parents and those children come together and look at one another, they know they can't turn the clock back. They can't go back, and they can't do it over. But they can look at each other and say, "We've both been wrong and we want forgiveness. Let's start over from here." I'll guarantee you Dad, Mom, that every one of your children will look at you and say, "We're going to go from here. The past is buried under the blood."

Pastor Ron Dryden, a marvelous minister of the Gospel, tells the following story of his daughter, Tawny:

> When she was a little girl, I was in sin. I didn't realize how much influence I had over my own children when they were young. One day I was shaving and my little girl was standing there beside me looking up at me. I finished and went outside.
>
> In a few moments, Tawny came outside crying with blood gushing down her neck. She had taken my shaving cream and put it on her face. Then she took the razor and tried to shave her face. She seriously cut her throat and neck.
>
> I grabbed her in my arms to rush her to the hospital. I was terrified: there was my little girl bleeding from her neck. It looked very serious. "Baby, why did you do that?" I asked her. That little girl looked up in my face and said, "Daddy, I want to be just like you."
>
> As I held my daughter the thought went through my mind: *I had a Christian father and look how I turned out because I rebelled against God. How is my daughter going to turn out if I won't live for God?*
>
> I saw the way I turned out and my dad had tried to set a good example; how would my daughter turn out when I wasn't setting any example at all for her with God?
>
> It so terrified me that I fell on my knees and asked Christ to forgive me and gave my heart to God.
>
> From that moment unto this I am saved because if my children are going to be like me, I want to set an example of how to follow the Lord Jesus Christ.

Years ago a preacher died, and as I looked at his body in the casket I remembered the words he had said to me weeks before as we had talked. He said, "I could die a happy man if my children would live for God." I looked from the casket to his three grown children sitting on the front row. Two of them were drunk and the other one was very far away from God.

I walked over and looked in those children's eyes. I shook their hands and told them, "The last thing your dad said to me was that he could die a happy man if he knew you would live for God." I don't know that they are, even now.

I know that there is a Satan out there that has disrupted our nation, our homes and our children. Kids today are caught in the very grip and vice of hell. They're trying to find a way out of it.

Love Makes the Difference

I have preached to convicts — big, strong, powerful convicts — who are in prison for murder and robbery and everything else. Many of them have stood up with tears in their eyes and said, "I came from a home where my daddy wouldn't tell me he loved me."

I don't mean for you to be some kind of mushy dad. I'm not talking about that. But Dad, I cannot tell you how your love can make your kid feel. Kids need to feel loved and nurtured so they can grow up emotionally healthy. Building boys and girls at home is easier than restoring and mending men and women.

I still remember the feel of my father's arm around my shoulder more than once when he could have taken a belt to me or could have put a fist in my face. Instead, he came to me in my drunken stupor, picked me up and said, "Dwight, I love you. Dwight, you're going to make it. Son, come on, I'm with you. You're going to make it."

Love makes the world go around, and the love of Jesus will really make that world go around for that child.

Parents, we can't turn back the clock. We can't go back and do things like we'd like to. But we can start right now by asking forgiveness. We can go to our children and say, "If we have failed you, and we have, will you forgive us?" God will heal that home. He'll bring those children around. But it's going to take a dad who is going to be a spiritual leader in that house.

A word to you who are divorced single parents. Your home ended in divorce. You're raising those children alone. I know that magnifies the problem. But I want to share with you a prayer that my mother prayed over me that has stuck to this day. "I plead the blood of Jesus over my children. I plead the blood over their lives."

Now the "old timers" used the expression "plead the blood" in their prayers to entreat the covering and protection of the blood of the Lamb of God, Jesus Christ, to rest on their children and loved ones. Just as the children of Israel applied the blood of the passover lamb to the sides and top of their door posts as a covering and protection from the Angel of Death (Ex. 12:12-14), we too ask the Lord for a covering and protection for our family and loved ones by symbolically applying or "pleading" the blood over their lives.

My dad, who died on October 4, 1990, and is now in heaven, always said to me when I'd close on the phone, "Son, if you ever need me, the door is always open and I'll be there." My son is married, has two children and works for us now as Director and General Manager of Dwight Thompson Ministries, but to this day when I talk to my boy on the phone I say, "Son, if you ever need me I'm here, and I can be there in a matter of minutes if you need me."

Mother and Daddy, it isn't enough to let the children be responsible.Those kids need your prayers at home. Start the family altar afresh and anew. Go in there and kneel down.

Daddy, don't be afraid to let those kids see your tears. Lay your hands upon them and let them hear you pray; let them feel the touch of your hand.

Dad, be alert. Even though you do everything you can for your kids, the last thing you say as those kids walk out the door is, "Devil, I plead the blood over my children's lives and you're not going to lay a hand upon my children in Jesus' name." Keep a wall of love around them.

5
Devil, You Can't Have My Children

5

Devil, You Can't Have My Children

A woman said to me some time ago, "I have nightmares, nightmares that my son is going to die in his sin." Have you ever had that nightmare? Is your son or daughter lost? Is your child away from God right now and the devil screaming at you, "See, I've got them. I'm going to kill them. I'm going to destroy them"?

Look again at Acts 16:31, please, if you'll take note of it: **Believe on the Lord Jesus Christ, and thou shalt be saved....**

What else did it say?

...and thy house! Remember that. You've already circled that Scripture, now list their names next to it because something is going to start right now, and your kids are going to get saved. Your prodigal is coming home to God. Pray that he will come to himself as the prodigal son's father in the Bible must have prayed.

A friend of mine, Norvel Hayes, lost everything he had in the early years of his life. He lost his wife; he lost his fortune. The only thing he had left was his daughter, Zona. And Satan began an attack to take away his only child. Her marriage disintegrated; her husband filed for divorce; she turned away from God.

It so disturbed Norvel, he said, that it broke his heart. He was terrified at what was happening to his daughter.

Norvel would go to his daughter and tell her, "Honey, you can't live the way you are living. I know you've had a bad blow, you don't understand it, and you may even charge God with it; but you can't go this route. You can't take it out on God; you can't take it out on your life." But the child went from bad to worse. She got involved with the wrong crowd and even started doing things that were very sad.

All Norvel could think about was that his daughter was going to die and go to hell. And to make matters worse, the devil would come in the middle of the night and say, "I'm going to kill her now. I got your wife. I got your home. I got your business and now I'm going to get your daughter; the only thing you've got left in your life, and I'm going to take her away from you."

Finally, tearfully, almost hysterically, he pleaded with his daughter, "Honey, you're killing me; you're killing me. I can't stand this any more. You're destroying me." He pleaded and cried and it seemed to make her rebel even more. One night when she walked out the door, Norvel cried to God. "Oh, God, the devil is killing my child. She may not be back tonight or tomorrow night. She's going around with the wrong crowd."

God said to him, "Why don't you turn her over to Me? Turn her over to Me and stand in faith on Acts 16:31. Stand right there and don't let anything cause your faith to waver."

Now our five senses influence how we think; we are often swayed by what we see. If we see something that is encouraging, then we are encouraged. But when you have a child who is lost and you see her going deeper in sin, it is difficult to stand on your faith and say, "My child is a disciple taught of the Lord, in obedience to the will of God, great shall be her peace and her composure." But Norvel said he started praying that prayer over his daughter when she was a rank sinner.

The devil would say, "You're a liar, Norvel Hayes. That Zona of yours is not a disciple taught of the Lord and is not in obedience to the will of God, and she certainly is not in peace and undisturbed composure."

The second thing the Lord told Norvel to do was "to love her. Don't try to understand her, don't try to figure her out and don't run up to her and say, 'You never will amount to anything.'" The Lord said, "Stand in your faith. Stand in your faith and do not compromise. Do not waver, but stand firmly upon Acts 16:31 and your daughter will be saved." The Lord encouraged Norvel, "Stand on Acts 2:39, **For the promise is unto you, and to your children, and to all that are afar off, even as many as the Lord our God shall call.**"

The next time Norvel's daughter was going out with friends that she shouldn't be with, Norvel went over to her, put his arm around her and said, "I love you." She said, "I love you, too, daddy," and got in the car and left. He said, "I didn't know if she would be back that night or the next night or the next."

That particular night the devil said — spoke right into his ear — "Tonight I'll kill her." Norvel said it made him so mad that he just stepped out onto the porch as that car disappeared in the night and lifted his voice up as loud as he could scream. He held his Bible in one hand and cupped his other hand near his mouth like a little megaphone and screamed so loudly that everyone in the neighborhood could hear. "Devil," he said, "Get your hands off my daughter." I guess somebody came out on the porch and wanted to know what was going on and Norvel told them, "I told the devil to get his hands off my daughter."

God had told him to "start praying the Word over her." Norvel said he would go in her room and pray over her clothes and over her bed. He would anoint with oil the place where she was going to sleep. And, he said, "It began to work. It began to work."

When people begin to stand on the Word of God, it will work. God's Word does not change because of a mountain. It does not change because of the circumstance. No mountain changes the Word of God, but the Word of God will blast any mountain into the sea. God's Word will change any circumstance. God's Word will get hold of your child. Standing on God's Word will bring that child to God. Norvel Hayes' daughter came to God!

Today Zona and her husband are back together serving God as ministers of the Gospel working alongside her father. When we had dinner with them last year, she looked across the table at us, tears rolling down her face, and she said, "I'd be in hell today if it wasn't for my dad's prayers. I am a product of prayer and the grace of God."

6
Mama, Hold Onto God

6
Mama, Hold Onto God

I remember, as a little kid, sitting on the front seat of the church with my little brother, Rex, and some of the other kids, and a little old lady who would stand up Sunday morning, Sunday night and in Wednesday night prayer service and would say the same thing — always the same request. I know it word for word. She would say, "Pray for my son; my son is lost and I don't know where he is. I haven't heard from him, but God has assured me according to Acts 16:31 that the Lord is going to save him, and I just want ya'll to pray for him. God's given me a promise. My son is going to be saved."

We'd see her getting up, and Rex and I and all the kids sitting there together would just say it with her. She'd give the same prayer request year after year after year. We kind of made fun of her — we were just little kids. So, I've known Acts 16:31 since I was six years old.

Then we got on up to be teenagers and that woman was still standing up. Do you know what she'd tell my dad? I can remember hearing it — it seems like a thousand times. That's what it seems like. "You know, God's going to save my son. I haven't heard from him now in fourteen years...." Then she said fifteen years...then sixteen. Well, after she hadn't heard from him in seventeen years and she was eighty years old, she was put into the hospital. The doctors said the little old woman was dying. Her daughter was the only one living other than the son — but she didn't actually know whether the son was living. But she kept standing on Acts 16:31.

It takes a lot of faith to believe God when your children are alcoholics or drug addicts and you don't know where they are and you haven't heard from them. It takes a lot of faith to stand up there and say, "You know, my children are going to be saved. The devil is not going to have my family."

This little old woman would get up in our church and say, "Pray for my boy. I don't know where he is but wherever he is just pray for him. God's going to save him. I'm standing on Acts 16:31." At the age of eighty she was in the hospital dying. She informed her daughter that she was not going to die until her boy came home because she had the promise that God was going to save him.

All of a sudden she spoke to her daughter and said, "He's on his way right now." The doctors seemed to think that, bless her little heart, her mind was now going because she was near death. She would look up every now and then and say, "He's almost here." Then she would say, "I know he's on the way." The daughter would say, "But you don't even know if he is alive or if he's dead. You haven't heard from him." But she kept standing on the Word.

That woman, at the age of eighty years of age, suddenly said, "He's here!" Sure enough; they turned and looked and in the doorway stood a ragged, unshaven, dirty man. It was her boy. He was now fifty-seven years old. Do you know what he did? He came over and put his head in his mother's lap. Six o'clock that evening, which was about four hours later, she went into eternity to meet God. But before she went out into eternity, she had the joy of leading her son — whom she had not even heard from in seventeen years — back to Jesus Christ. He is a born-again child of God! Man, if that won't do it, nothing will.

Later when he testified he told my dad, "I don't understand what happened. I was an alcoholic and had been in Houston for years." It was an awful story, but he was nothing more than a washed-up piece of broken, emaciated humanity. He said that night he didn't even remember what happened. "All I know," he said, "was I found myself in the train yard. Something kind of helped me and tugged on me to get into this open car. I laid down, and the next thing I remember something impressed me to get out of the car.

"It seemed like I started walking from the Santa Fe depot in Fort Worth, which would have been about two miles, to the St. Joseph Hospital. Every time I made the wrong turn, something would direct me another way."

I believe God just said, "It's time," and sent a couple of angels there to put him on that boxcar and head him to Fort Worth. There are a thousand cars there. He could have gotten on a train that was going to Ottawa, Canada; but not this time. His mother had a hold of God. She had a pact with God. There was a covenant with God.

I want to tell you something and don't ever forget it: if you're born again, you're a covenant child, and you've got rights, and what affects you affects God. He loves you very much. As sparrows fall from the heaven, and God attends the funeral of every sparrow that falls, and the hairs on your head are numbered, how much more is He concerned about your children for whom He sent His Son to die? He's going to save those children, but it's going to take you standing in faith for them. You see, their faith won't work right now, but yours will. Don't be discouraged. Remember, God loves them more than you do.

God blocked that man for seventeen years from going to hell. I know what it was. Every time that man would take a wrong turn a big angel would stand there and say, "No, no, you're going the wrong way. Get on over there." The angel kept shoving him. He said, "I was standing in front of the hospital and I don't even know how I got to the elevator or who opened it. I don't remember punching any floor. All

I know is that I got off on this floor and I walked down these halls and I was standing in this room and something shoved me inside."

I can see one angel saying to another angel, "You want to push him, or should I? Oh, let's do it together." They shoved him inside and God took over, because God had one little old lady who for seventeen years held on to God's Word for her son. He was saved. He was born again into the kingdom of God. *God saved him.* God saved him. God honored His Word.

7
Keep the Light On
and the Table Ready

7

Keep the Light On
and the Table Ready

My wife, Zonelle, came from a preacher's home: a good, godly preacher's home. Her younger brother, Ronnie, eight years younger than she, was one of the orneriest youths that ever came down the pike. I was preaching a revival in Albuquerque, New Mexico, years ago for her dad. Well, Ronnie was away from God. I'd see Ronnie during that time and he'd be high on drugs. Sister Greer, Zonelle's mama, would walk the floor every night of that revival, praying for Ronnie — didn't know where he was — but praying for him, watching out for Ronnie. She would walk the floor. "Devil, you're not going to have Ronnie. I'm claiming the Word of God for my boy. I believe God's going to save my son." She'd walk the floor like a little old caged lioness. She wouldn't turn loose of the Word of God. She'd get a hold of the Word and say, "Devil, get your hands off of my Ronnie."

Do you know what else his mama did? She kept the light turned on inside his room, every night, so he could see it on from the outside if he came by the house. She left the door unlocked and made sure Ronnie could get in. When we sat down at the table to eat, she set a place for Ronnie. She set aside food for Ronnie and made sure nobody ate Ronnie's food. She wanted Ronnie to know, just in case he came home, that there was food saved for him. She'd put it on the stove with Ronnie's name on it, just in case he came home. Nobody sat in Ronnie's chair; nobody slept in Ronnie's bed. Ronnie had a waterbed. Can you imagine a waterbed? She made sure that waterbed was full, the sheets were clean, and that enough covers were on the bed just in case he showed up.

When I would see that precious mama walking the floor, agonizing over that little lost boy, it aggravated me so much to see her heart so broken. Sometimes I got so mad at Ronnie that I wanted to take him out into the back yard and give him a good old one-two and let him know why he shouldn't be killing his mama. I'd make him a Christian in two minutes! He'd be a live one or a dead one, but I'd make him a Christian one way or the other. Well, see, I was wrong. I didn't know it then, but I was just agonizing for his mama.

Zonelle was standing in faith with her mama for Ronnie and her daddy was standing in faith for Ronnie, and Ronnie would come in and go to his waterbed. That irritated me. I said to Zonelle one night, "That's killing your mama. It's killing her. It's breaking my heart to see your mother like this. That boy knows better than that."

I learned a valuable lesson through all of that. Parents, you may not realize why they are doing it. You may not understand them, but keep on loving them. Keep the meal and the table ready. Keep the door open. Keep the light on. Let them know when they come in — it doesn't matter if they are the biggest junkie in town — there is one place in town that that junkie can go, and it's called home. You can bridge the generation gap with love. Keep holding on to God for them. Keep your arms held out to them and say, "I love you."

I remember as a rebellious teenager that I left home and went away. When my daddy found me, he put his arms around me — and I can hear it to this day — and he said, "Son, I don't know why you're doing what you're doing, but I want you to know one thing, together we're going to lick it; whatever it is, I'm going to stand with you. Whatever it is, I want you to know that you are welcome at home." I know I am a born-again child of God because my daddy didn't put a fist in my face when he could have, but he reached down in the pit where I was and said, "Son, I believe in you. You're going to make it."

Teenagers reading this book, I believe in you, and you are going to make it. I don't care how many mistakes you've made, you're going to make it. You're going to make it.

Sister Greer just kept loving him. She didn't scream at him and say, "You no account person, you're never going to amount to anything. I don't know why you're living." She didn't talk like that to him. She kept loving him. Whatever happened, she kept loving him.

Parents, keep loving them. If they're so spaced out they don't know which way they're going, you keep loving them. You keep holding on to God. You keep binding the power of the devil. You say, "Devil, you get your hands off my children in the name of Jesus." Then keep standing and standing and standing.

One night during the revival when I was preaching, Ronnie came in and sat down in the back row. (Now, the day before this night, the Scripture in Romans 16:20 became so real to Zonelle and her mom. We knew the time was near. **And the God of peace shall bruise Satan under your feet shortly.**) The revival had been going on for weeks. All of a sudden, you know how mamas are, Sister Greer didn't even have to turn around, her spirit told her that her boy had come in the building that night.

God bless mamas. There's no one like a mama. I know daddies love their sons, but nobody can feel what that mama can feel. I believe that God used to tell my mother things, and she knew what I was doing a hundred miles away. Mamas just know.

75

That church was packed and Ronnie was sitting in the back. I conveniently switched my sermon and started preaching on the prodigal son.

I can still see that boy: about 6'3", coming down that aisle even before I finished my sermon, sobbing, crying big old tears. Little Sister Greer knew he was coming. She was saying, "Thank You, Jesus. Thank You, Jesus. Thank You, Jesus. Thank You, Jesus." When Ronnie went by Sister Greer, she got right up behind him and walked to the altar with Ronnie. That night, still at midnight, Ronnie was flat on his back, praying in a heavenly language, and the Lord came down and set him free from his drugs. Set him free!

Ronnie is saved, filled with the Holy Ghost and serving God today, because one mama would not turn loose of her boy.

That's the authority of the Word of God. Though your son or daughter may be as far from God as you think they can get, that doesn't mean the devil has them signed, sealed and delivered into the pit of hell, because he can't get around a mama's prayer. God's going to put up roadblocks on the road to hell, and I believe the angels of mercy are going to be extended to protect that man or that woman or that boy or that girl until they are able to come to God. Why? Because you belong to God and they belong to you, and what concerns you concerns God. **The Lord will perfect that which concerneth me** (Ps. 138:8). Stand on the Word. Just stand on the Word. The Word says, **Believe on the Lord Jesus Christ, and thou shalt be saved...AND THY HOUSE** (Acts 16:31)!

I want you to adopt this policy now. I don't care what the physical evidence tells you; I don't care if your eyes still tell you that your child comes home drunk. Maybe you have had to drag them to bed and put them in bed with their clothes on. Maybe you have had to clean up the mess after they have thrown up all over, and you are sick to your stomach. Daddy, maybe you have gotten in your car and driven all over trying to find your children. Maybe you have walked the floor many nights and all the while the devil says, "I'm going to kill your child." Stand firm and say, "No, you're not, devil. God's going to save my child." Call those things that be not as though they were. (Rom. 4:17.) Daddy, don't you give up. Mama, you hang in there, dear.

It doesn't take any faith for you if they are saved and sitting in church, but when the devil has absolutely paraded his work in their lives before your eyes, it takes another kind of faith to stand there in the face of that evidence. The physical evidence says, "I am going to kill that child. I have that child." But your faith says, "You may have him right now, but pretty soon God is going to have him, and I'm not going to be deterred in my faith, nor will I waver. I'm not going to waver." Say that out loud even as you're reading this, "I'm not going to waver. I'm not going to waver. My children shall be saved." Say it again.

You can start believing God for your children to be saved...and saved right away! Stand on the Word for your children.

Here are some Scriptures you can stand on:

For the Son of man came to seek and to save that which was lost.

Luke 19:10 AMP

For the god of this world has blinded the unbelievers' minds (that they should not discern the truth), preventing them from seeing the illuminating light of the Gospel of the glory of Christ, the Messiah, Who is the image and likeness of God.

2 Corinthians 4:4 AMP

Then He said to His disciples, The harvest is indeed plentiful, but the laborers are few. So pray the Lord of

the harvest to force out and thrust laborers into His harvest.

Matthew 9:37,38 AMP

For I will be merciful and gracious toward their sins and I will remember their deeds of unrighteousness no more.

Hebrews 8:12 AMP

And there is salvation in and through no one else, for there is no other name under heaven given among men by and in which we must be saved.

Acts 4:12 AMP

If we [freely] admit that we have sinned and confess our sins, He is faithful and just [true to His own nature and promises] and will forgive our sins (dismiss our lawlessness) and continuously cleanse us from all unrighteousness — everything not in conformity to His will in purpose, thought and action.

1 John 1:9 AMP

But to as many as did receive and welcome Him, He gave the authority [power, privilege, right] to become the children of God, that is, to those who believe in — adhere to, trust in and rely on — His name.

John 1:12 AMP

Behold, I stand at the door and knock; if any one hears and listens to and heeds My voice and opens the door, I will come in to him and will eat with him, and he [shall eat] with Me.

Revelation 3:20 AMP

8
Train Your Children in the Way They Should Go

8

Train Your Children in the Way They Should Go

Our children are without a doubt the most precious possession that God has given us in this world. I might say, also as a grandfather, that we not only have the glorious and precious privilege of rearing our children but also of being a grandparent. I'm enjoying that role very, very much.

I realize that you have children or grandchildren or someone in your life that you're responsible for. We realize that our children, our teenagers, our grandchildren are faced with tremendous pressures. The pressures upon our teenagers today are far greater than the pressures that were upon me when I was a teenager. I have heard people make the statement, even from the pulpit, that, "There's no more pressure on teenagers today than there was pressure on me when I was a teenager."

I simply cannot accept that. Our teenagers have been thrust into a society that is open and promiscuous. They are inundated, if you will, from television with every kind of value system that opposes itself to God. Every magazine they pick up, every influence they get from the media says it's cool to be with the in crowd that is involved in every kind of standard and value that is directly opposite from the Word of God.

This book is born out of a heart, not only of a minister of the Gospel, not only from the heart of a born-again Christian, not only from the heart of an evangelist, but it is from the heart of a father, the heart of a grandfather.

God is opening our eyes. It's almost as though the veil has been torn apart. He has shown us that as parents every one of us has been somewhat brainwashed into believing that we should take our hands off of our children — let them make their own decisions, let them go their own way, because whatever will be will be. I cannot find that in the Scriptures.

The Word of God first of all says, **Train up a child in the way he should go: and when he is old, he will not depart from it** (Prov. 22:6). God has a plan for your children. Let me give you some truths from the Scriptures.

> **And all your [spiritual] children shall be disciples — taught of the Lord [and obedient to His will]; and great shall be the peace and undisturbed composure of your children.**
>
> **Isaiah 54:13 AMP**

That's a promise I pray over my family every day. This is what I do as a preacher of the Gospel. I pray this every day over my family:

> **...for I will contend with him who contends with you, and I will give safety to your children and ease them.**
>
> **Isaiah 49:25 AMP**

> **For this is the covenant the Lord has made with me. His Spirit is upon me who writes the law of God inwardly in my heart. And His words which He has put in my mouth, shall not depart out of my mouth, [listen, here's the plan of God:] Or out of the mouth of my children, or out of the mouth of my children's children henceforth and forever.**
>
> **Isaiah 59:21 AMP (paraphrased)**

This was not the plan of man. This was the plan of God. The plan of God was to bless the seed of Abraham, to bless the seed of Isaac and to bless the seed of Jacob. God's plan is not only now for me, Dwight Thompson, but it is also for my children. It is also for my grandchildren. It is for my seed because I am a child of God.

There is a pronouncement of blessing. There is a benefit in that Christian lineage that passes down. God's intention was not only for me to be saved, but for my seed to be saved. I want you to get that in your spirit. It is God's plan, God's desire, God's will for your children to be saved, every one of them.

> But the mercy of the Lord is from everlasting to everlasting upon them that fear him, and his righteousness unto children's children.
>
> **Psalm 103:17**

> But we behaved gently when we were among you, like a devoted mother nursing and cherishing her own children. So, being thus tenderly and affectionately desirous of you, we continued to share with you not only God's good news (the Gospel) but also our own lives as well, for you had become so very dear to us.
>
> **1 Thessalonians 2:7,8 AMP**

Did you get that? Like a devoted mother nursing and cherishing her own children.

> Lo, children are an heritage of the Lord: and the fruit of the womb is his reward. As arrows are in the hand of a mighty man; so are children of the youth. Happy is the man that hath his quiver full of them . . . .
>
> **Psalm 127:3-5**

The Bible says children are a heritage from the Lord and happy, blessed, and fortunate is the man whose quiver is filled with them. The word "quiver" means a case in which arrows are kept. The Bible said that happy is the man whose quiver is filled with them: children.

> Fear not, for I am with you; I will bring your offspring from the east [where they are dispersed], and gather you from the west.
>
> **Isaiah 43:5 AMP**

> **Thus says the Lord: Refrain your voice from
> weeping, and your eyes from tears; for your work shall
> be rewarded, says the Lord; and [your children] shall
> return from the enemy's land.**
>
> **Jeremiah 31:16 AMP**

God has a plan, a divine destiny for your children, a destiny.

I believe, without a doubt, that there is an atmosphere and an environment that is very conducive to influencing our children either for God or for Satan.

Our young people today are barraged with voices that are influencing much of what is taking place in America. What can we do in order to provide the proper influence for them? How can we give them proper role models?

> **Train up a child in the way he should go: and when
> he is old, he will not depart from it.**
>
> **Proverbs 22:6**

You say, "Dwight, this is not present tense faith. It's future faith."

In my opinion, that is for the present. It's a lot easier for me to have faith for the future when I realize in the present that I have allowed my family and my children and now my grandchildren to hear about faith in the present. The reason I can put so much faith in this Scripture for the future is because I'm doing something about it in the present.

Your Children Imitate You

Children are imitators of their parents. The strongest influence in your children's life is you, the parent.

Dad, I know you know this but I feel led of God to remind you: your son is watching you more closely, probably, than anyone else in his life. As early as age two and three, your son is already drawing his opinions from you.

Did you know that? He's already learning how to do things you do. He's learning to react the way you react about certain things. Even though he may not express it, your every action, every deed, every word, every reaction to situations, psychologists tell us, makes an indelible impression in the life of your son.

I remember vividly one time when Zonelle and I were walking in a park. A five-year-old boy was with another boy, and the five year old was cursing. He was using as vile a language as you could hear any man ever use. That boy had heard that somewhere. It wasn't long until we heard a boy's name called, and he turned around. He was only a few feet away, and we saw a man and woman coming toward him. We heard that father and mother, both of them, yell at that child in the filthiest language you could imagine. There was no mystery to be solved. It was obvious where that five-year-old child had learned to curse. Children are imitators of their parents.

Many, many years ago in Atlanta, Georgia, I saw something that absolutely shocked me. Outside a church building in Atlanta a grown man, watching a black man enter the church, said quietly to a person near him, "Why are these black people coming here to the church?" (only he used terrible slang language).

I walked over to him — it got all over me for a minute — and I asked, "Why should they not come to church with us?"

He said, "Because I hate them."

"Has a black person ever done anything to you in your life?" I asked him.

"Well, no." he said.

I said, "Have you or anybody in your family ever been accosted by a black person? Has a black person ever been rude to you in your entire life?"

"No."

I said, "Then give me one reason why you hate them."

"Because," he said, "well, my daddy hated them."

"Do you mean you hate today strictly because your father hated? Did you ever figure out why your father hated them?" I asked.

He said, "No. The only thing I could figure out was that his daddy hated them." Do you see the point? No one influences children like parents. This man hated because his daddy hated.

I remember hearing a true story about a man who started teaching his son how to drink when he became a teenager, at age thirteen. Instead of teaching that teenager about the dangers of that filthy thing called liquor, he said, "I'm going to teach my child how to be responsible in his drinking." So he always kept a bottle of liquor in the refrigerator. Little by little he taught the boy to drink — always responsibly. It was always right there in the refrigerator.

One day he got a call at his office telling him that his son was in the hospital. He rushed to the hospital, but when he got there, he was told his son had died. The boy had been driving while drunk and had, had an accident.

The father went into a rage. "That boy is only sixteen. He's under age. I'm going to find the store in this county that sold him that liquor. I'll sell my house. I'll sell everything I've got until I find the person in this town who sold my boy the liquor, sold it to a minor." That's what he said.

When he got home, he went to the refrigerator to get his nightly drink to settle his nerves and there was a note where the liquor bottle used to be. The note read, "Dad, don't worry about me. I took the liquor. You taught me how to drink and I know how to drink responsibly." He signed his name. That dad fell on his knees and said, "I am the man who taught him how to drink."

Moral restraints have been thrown off in our society today, because most homes do not know how to even teach children morality, much less about God. They've been given over to the influences of the world.

Children are imitators of their parents. Their values come from the home. The value systems that are formed in their lives are set by parents and the environment of that home.

9
Choose To Influence
Your Children for God

9

Choose To Influence
Your Children for God

Children are either products of a godly environment or products of an ungodly environment. Research done on people today who are alcoholics has determined that their role models in life were family members who were alcoholics. So on it goes. We must realize that those few years that we have those children are the most important years of their life.

I remember in Miami, Florida, many years ago we were preaching a revival. A man, who was a member of a very strong crime family, got saved in one of the meetings. As a result there were over twenty other members in that family who also came to Jesus Christ. He told the story later that every one of these children had been taught crime by him. It was handed down by him. These criminal children were the product of a criminal environment.

I was raised in a Christian home and I thank God for it. It was not only a Christian home, but as I've said, a Pentecostal preacher's home. I'm so honored to have been raised in that home. But did you know my father being saved did not save me? My mother being saved did not save me? My father being a Christian did not save me? But what they did was they created a Christian environment that influenced my life.

My father did not always preach at me and he did not talk down to me. He did more than that. Read this carefully. It will help you. This is the mark of an environment. When I was a child I can remember my father prayed. I can remember my mother prayed. I can remember the first thing my dad would do when he would get out of the bed every morning would be to begin to quote Psalm 103. It was as common to him as getting up in the morning. I knew that Psalm, probably most of it, before I was ten years old. He would quote it, and I can quote it to this day.

> **Bless the Lord, O my soul: and all that is within me, bless his holy name. Bless the Lord, O my soul, and forget not all his benefits: Who forgiveth all thine iniquities; who healeth all thy diseases; Who redeemeth thy life from destruction; who crowneth thee with lovingkindness and tender mercies; Who satisfieth thy mouth with good things; so that thy youth is renewed like the eagle's.**
>
> **Psalm 103:1-5**

My dad would quote that every morning. Do you see what point I'm trying to make? I remember this godly environment.

Another thing I remember was my mother praying. I remember her praying so well. She was one of these prayer intercessors who didn't believe much in five-minute prayers. My mother was one of these two-hour pray-ers. Every day of her life she put herself in that little closet in our house, and she prayed. When it came time to pray, the house got quiet. That's environment. Now again, that environment did not automatically mean I was born again. But at least it created a spiritual environment that let me sense and feel the presence and the power of God.

The values of parents and the habits of parents will be embraced by the children.

I remember my little brother and I used to stand up on apple crates in the yard and he'd preach, then I'd preach. Sometimes we'd sneak across the yard and get into the church when Daddy wasn't there. I would sit way out in the empty church building. Rex would get up behind the pulpit on a chair and pretend he was preaching. He knew how to give an altar call! He'd ask me if I wanted to come to God. So I'd get up, I was five or six years old, and I'd come down there and give my heart to God.

Then I'd let him get out there and be the sinner and I'd preach. We learned how to do that when we were quite young. Being raised like that had an influence on our lives.

Then there was my mother's praying. Many times my mama would say to me, "Son, when you can't find the answers and you don't know where to turn, when nothing you try comes to pass, you get on your knees. You can touch God. God will answer prayer." So I believe in prayer.

We prayed in the morning; we quoted the Word in the morning; we prayed at the table; we prayed at church. All of this created a spiritual knowledge of God.

Even as a child when I was three or four on up through my teen years, I could not go to sleep at night until I got down on my knees and prayed. I couldn't pray just lying in bed. It was important to me to get down on my knees and kneel before God. Even though the prayer may not take one minute, it was important to me that I exercised this prayer posture, because that's the way I was taught.

I want to impress upon you that this did not save me, but it created a godly environment. Everything that goes on in the home is part of the environment.

There were rules in our house. Nobody came into our house smoking. Nobody came into our house cursing. Nobody was allowed to come in our house and tell a dirty joke. It was more than a house; it was a place dedicated to God, just like the church. My father demanded reverence. I mean, he demanded it. That environment had an effect on me.

My home is the same way. I don't allow dirty jokes in my house. I don't allow conduct unbecoming a born-again Christian to be carried on in my house. I can't keep people from doing it outside, but I can prevent it from coming inside, because our home is dedicated to God.

It's important that you create a godly atmosphere; and if you do, the most rank sinner who walks in there will reverence your house. Why? It is a house of God — I'm not talking about a church building — I'm talking about your home. Your children will learn to reverence that home dedicated to God.

Precious parents and grandparents.... There may be grandparents reading this and saying, "Dwight, my children are not Christians. I'm worried about them and their children."

Grandma and Grandad, you have an opportunity to create a godly spiritual environment so that every time the children come over with the grandchildren those children and grandchildren experience a spiritual godly environment, a place of peace.

Children Are Marked by Example

This may be the most important statement of all. Our children are marked by our example more than by anything else...more than anything. They are marked by example. It's one thing to tell your children what to do. It's one thing to instruct them. That's good. It's one thing to teach them the Bible. That's good. That's important. It's one thing to teach them how to say a prayer.

That's one thing. But it's another thing altogether to teach them by example. It isn't what we say but what we are. And what we are is what we do. What we do is really what we are. In other words, it's the old adage, actions speak louder than words.

I remember reading a piercing story about a little boy who wanted to go to a movie. He said, "Mama, you've taught me what's really important and I want to tell you that I think that church isn't very important."

Surprised, his mother looked at him and asked, "What do you mean church isn't very important?"

This was his answer. "On Sunday when I go to church you give me two nickels. But on Saturday when I want to go to the movies you give me $2.00." What an indictment! I think we really need to stop and think about how the lifestyle we live before our children affects their desire for the things of God.

It can cause them to choose God's way and God's lifestyle rather than the lifestyle of the world. We teach them by our convictions and we teach them by example. As a child of God and as a preacher of the Gospel, I believe my personal commitment to the house of God speaks louder to my children than anything I say.

I think the nicest compliment my children have ever said to me is, "Dad, what we love and appreciate about you and Mom both is that you not only preach it in the pulpit, but we see you live it in our private life, in our home." Your example has a greater, stronger impact upon your children than anything else does.

The Bible clearly teaches us to be an example.

...be thou an example of the believers, in word, in conversation, in charity, in spirit, in faith, in purity.

1 Timothy 4:12

First, Paul says to be an example in word, everything that you say. That's important. Second, he says to be an example in conduct. It isn't enough to tell your children to go to church. It isn't enough. You really can't expect them to go if you don't go. "I send them, Dwight. I see that they get there," you say.

More important than seeing that your children get to church with a neighbor or on a church bus or any other way is for you to take them yourself. Don't expect that child to serve God if you don't. Mama, Daddy, don't expect it. Don't expect them to serve God if you won't serve God.

You say, "I'm too busy." There will come a time in your life when you will hear your own children say, "I'm too busy for God. I'm too busy for the church." I think the greatest testimonies are the ones I see every time I'm in the pulpit and I see a father and mother leading their children down to the front, sitting on the pew — teaching them not only in word, but by example.

Paul said to be an example in word, in conduct, and in love. Let them see your love in every situation. And then Paul said to be an example in spirit, in faith and in purity. Everyone of these denotes character. Paul is saying, "Be an example in your character."

Commitment Produces Christ-like Behavior

Here are a few things about character Zonelle and I have learned and lived by in setting an example for our children. God spoke this to Zonelle and me: You take care of your character, and I'll take care of your reputation. Also remember: it is not who you are that holds you back in life; it is who you think you are. Crisis does not build character, but it does reveal character.

Do you know what a commitment is? A commitment is something that you not only do, but you are. When you make a commitment, that commitment is not moved or changed because of how you feel. To commit one's self is to do some act or make some declaration which may bind the person in honor, good faith or consistency to pursue a certain course of conduct and then to adhere to it.

I've made a commitment to do what God says regarding teaching my children. I have made a commitment to adhere to this course of conduct. I've made a commitment to truth. I've made a commitment to God for my children — not that it will save them — but I've made a commitment to God to influence my children. I've made a commitment to the Bible. I've made a commitment to prayer. I've made a commitment to church. I've made a commitment to spiritual leadership. My point is this: it creates the environment in which my children can be marked for God.

It's Not too Late

If you say, "Dwight, I didn't have that opportunity. I wasn't raised in a Christian home. I didn't raise my kids as Christians. What can I do?"

You can take everything I've said and you can do something about it. If you were not a Christian when you were raising your children and now you are, there's still a lot you can do.

Even though your children are grown and they haven't seen you live this life because you didn't know it, don't be disheartened. You can do it now in so many ways. You can pray. You can stand on the Word of God. Use the Scriptures I've given you in this book.

Be a friend to them. Even though you're a parent, you can also be one of their best friends.

The most important thing of all is to be an example. Maybe they have seen you live for the devil, now they're going to see you live for God. They're going to see such a difference in your life. You're going to touch them by your example.

A lot of people have told me, "Dwight, my children don't want to have anything to do with God."

That's all right; let them go their way. But still be an example to them. How we live is sometimes the only Bible people read.

Finally, have a home full of love. No matter what they do, no matter how far from God they go, no matter how much they rebel against God, keep that love flowing.

I believe with you that with these simple, little instructions, God is going to get you on a road with your children like you've never had before. And they will come to God. I'm standing in faith with you right now, even as I write this.

Look at the story of Rahab from the book of Joshua.

When the spies went into Jericho, they were in a dangerous position. The Israelites had to take this major city first or its inhabitants, the Canaanites, would kill them before they went any further into the land. The spies entered the city and knocked on a door right inside the wall; the woman invited them in. She recognized they were not Canaanites as soon as they stepped inside. Someone else knocked on the door so she took the two men up on her roof and hid them under the flax that she was drying. Then she went back and answered the door. There stood some Canaanites. They asked, "Have you seen two Hebrew men?" She lied and sent the Canaanites in another direction. She waited until that night, then went up on top of the wall and began to talk to the men.

She said, "I have heard about the God you serve. I have heard about the things He has done." (Remember, **faith cometh by hearing** [Rom. 10:17].) She feared God. "He is going to give you this city; but please promise me that when you take this city you won't kill me."

They responded, "We won't kill you. You have put your life on the line for us."

Then she let them down by a cord through the window: for her house was upon the town wall, and she dwelt upon the wall.

> And the men said unto her, We will be blameless of
> this thine oath which thou has made us swear.
>
> Behold, when we come into the land, thou shalt
> bind this line of scarlet thread in the window which
> thou didst let us down by: and thou shalt bring thy
> father, and thy mother, and thy brethren, and all thy
> father's household, home unto thee.
>
> And it shall be, that whosoever shall go out of the
> doors of thy house into the street, his blood shall be
> upon his head, and we will be guiltless: and whosoever
> shall be with thee in the house, his blood shall be on
> our head, if any hand be upon him.
>
> And if thou utter this our business, then we will be
> quit of thine oath which thou hast made us to swear.
>
> And she said, According unto your words, so be it.
> And she sent them away, and they departed: and she
> bound the scarlet line in the window.
>
> Joshua 2:15,17-21

They told her to take the bright scarlet line, or cord, and
hang it in her window. Then when they came into the city to
take it, they would see the cord and it would distinguish
her house from all the others.

She said something that shows she is saved. She said,
"Can I bring my father and mother, my brothers, sisters,
aunts, uncles, cousins, nephews and nieces...*my household*?"

They said, "Yes."

When someone receives Christ, they are so happy that
the first thing they usually say is, "Can you agree with me
for my husband (or wife) and my children? And here is a
list of my family members...."

Look at Joshua 6:23,25:

> And the young men that were spies went in, and
> brought out Rahab, and her father, and her mother, and
> her brethren, and all that she had; and they brought out

99

all her kindred, and left them without the camp of Israel.

And Joshua saved Rahab the harlot alive, and her father's household, and all that she had; and she dwelleth in Israel even unto this day; because she hid the messengers, which Joshua sent to spy out Jericho.

Rahab remains as an example of a woman who, because of her faith, was not only pardoned but was raised to a position of honor. She is commended in the New Testament for her faith.

By faith the harlot Rahab perished not with them that believed not, when she had received the spies with peace.

Hebrews 11:31

Likewise also was not Rahab the harlot justified by works, when she had received the messengers, and had sent them out another way?

James 2:25

God will save your family because of your prayers, if you stand in faith.

10
Now, Lead Them to the Lord

10
Now, Lead Them to the Lord

We have gone through the Scriptures. We now know how to claim our family, how to influence our children for God; how to stand in the gap for them. I'm believing with you that all your family is coming to God. I expect your family to be saved.

Now, if your loved one would come to you and say, "Please lead me to the Lord Jesus Christ," would you know how to do it? Do you know how to tell somebody to be born again? Do you know where the Scriptures are in the Word of God? Let me help you right here.

Here are really the ABCs of salvation.

First, in order to be saved they have to acknowledge that they are a sinner.

> **For all have sinned, and come short of the glory of God.**
>
> **Romans 3:23**

> **All we like sheep have gone astray; we have turned every one to his own way; and the Lord hath laid on him the iniquity of us all.**
>
> **Isaiah 53:6**

> **For whosoever shall keep the whole law, and yet offend in one point, he is guilty of all.**
>
> **James 2:10**

In other words, if you've broken one law, you've broken them all.

But glory, honour, and peace, to every man that worketh good, to the Jew first, and also to the Gentile: For there is no respect of persons with God.

Romans 2:10,11

Number two, they must believe in Christ.

And they said, Believe on the Lord Jesus Christ, and thou shalt be saved, and thy house.

Acts 16:31

I came not to call the righteous, but sinners to repentance.

Luke 5:32

I tell you Nay: but, except ye repent, ye shall all likewise perish.

Luke 13:3

Or despisest thou the riches of his goodness and forbearance and longsuffering; not knowing that the goodness of God leadeth thee to repentance?

Romans 2:4

For God so loved the world, that he gave his only begotten Son, that whosoever believeth in him should not perish, but have everlasting life.

John 3:16

The third part is they must confess Christ as their Savior.

That if thou shalt confess with thy mouth the Lord Jesus, and shalt believe in thine heart that God hath raised him from the dead, thou shalt be saved.

Romans 10:9

Whosoever shall confess that Jesus is the Son of God, God dwelleth in him, and he in God.

1 John 4:15

And many that believed came, and confessed, and shewed their deeds.

Acts 19:18

> **If we confess our sins, he is faithful and just to forgive us our sins, and to cleanse us from all unrighteousness.**
>
> **1 John 1:9**

That's the basic plan: A, B, C. That's how to lead people to Christ. A: acknowledge self as sinner. B: believe in Christ. C: confess Christ as Savior.

Answer Their Questions

Some people will still have questions.

They may say to you, "I am too great a sinner. How can I be saved?"

> **For the Son of man is come to seek and to save that which was lost.**
>
> **Luke 19:10**

> **This is a faithful saying, and worthy of all acceptation, that Christ Jesus came into the world to save sinners; of whom I am chief.**
>
> **1 Timothy 1:15**

> **All that the Father giveth me shall come to me; and him that cometh to me I will in no wise cast out.**
>
> **John 6:37**

> **Wherefore he is able also to save them to the uttermost that come unto God by him, seeing he ever liveth to make intercession for them.**
>
> **Hebrews 7:25**

If someone feels he is too great a sinner, read those verses of Scripture to him.

What about that precious one who says, "I'm afraid I can't hold out. I don't think I could live that life." You've got good news for him.

> **Now unto him that is able to keep you from falling, and to present you faultless before the presence of his glory with exceeding joy, To the only wise God our**

Saviour, be glory and majesty, dominion and power, both now and for ever. Amen.

Jude 24,25

For the which cause I also suffer these things: nevertheless I am not ashamed: for I know whom I have believed, and am persuaded that he is able to keep that which I have committed unto him against that day.

2 Timothy 1:12

Wherefore he is able also to save them to the uttermost that come unto God by him, seeing he ever liveth to make intercession for them.

Hebrews 7:25

Encourage your loved ones with these Scriptures. Then lead them in the sinner's prayer.

Dear Lord Jesus, I call upon You to have mercy on my life. I'm a sinner and I need God. I believe that You, Jesus, are the Christ, the Son of the Living God.

From this moment on, I promise with God's help and grace to serve You. I turn my back on sin. I forsake sin. I'll live for You, Jesus. I'm going to follow You, Jesus.

I believe right now that Your blood cleanses me from all my sins. I know at this moment my name is being written in heaven. Thank You, Jesus. Amen. Amen. Amen.

Dwight Thompson has become one of the most powerful preachers of our time. Known world-wide for his legendary ability to captivate and move an audience, he has dedicated his ministry to salvation and deliverance through Jesus Christ.

The elements which make his message unforgettable include humor, compassion, deeply rooted biblical convictions and unique ways of illustrating the meaning of scriptural phrases, parables and promises.

Thompson has traveled around the world as an evangelist, preaching to millions and leading thousands to Jesus Christ. His crusades frequently launch long-lasting revivals.

With his ability to communicate the Gospel with power and charisma, he touches countless lives. Through a series of crusades in one Southern California city, several thousand people accepted Christ.

In Bombay, India, 22 churches had their beginnings in a Dwight Thompson Crusade. With the aid of Dwight Thompson World Outreach Ministries, numerous church buildings, an evangelistic training center and a Christian school were constructed in Bombay.

Before becoming an evangelist, Thompson was an associate pastor with his father, James Curtis Thompson. He then began his ministry in 1963 in Fort Worth, Texas, at Faith Temple.

Today, he is married and has two children and five grandchildren. His wife, Zonelle, travels with him nationwide. Zonelle also speaks at many women's seminars. His son, Dwight, Jr., is the Executive Director of Dwight Thompson Ministries and produces and directs the "Dwight Thompson" television program, broadcast throughout the United States and around the world.

Dwight and Zonelle Thompson are also frequent guest hosts of the "Praise the Lord" program on the Trinity Broadcasting Network (TBN).

An accomplished singer, he has recorded nine albums and uses his musical ministry to enhance his message.

Truly, Dwight Thompson is a man with a call on his life and a commitment in his heart.

To contact the author,
write:

Dwight Thompson
P. O. Box 1122
Downey, California 90240

*Please include your prayer requests
or comments when you write.*

Additional copies of this book are available
from your local bookstore or from:

Harrison House
P. O. Box 35035
Tulsa, Oklahoma 74153

In Canada contact:

Word Alive
P. O. Box 284
Niverville, Manitoba
CANADA ROA 1EO

The Harrison House Vision

Proclaiming the truth and power
Of the Gospel of Jesus Christ
With excellence;

Challenging Christians to
Live victoriously,
Grow spiritually,
Know God intimately.